LET GOD BE PRESENT

Uncovering the Will, Courage, and Persistence to Truly Connect

MATTHEW D. BROUGH

LET GOD BE PRESENT

By Matthew D. Brough

Edited by Lauren Craft, www.sharpeyeedits.net.

CONTENTS

INTRODUCTION

So much writing about God assumes that we want more of God, but I am not convinced that we all have that desire. Even as a pastor, I have not always wanted to be in God's presence.

I remember singing the words of Psalm 42 when I was a teenager and I always cringed. "As the Deer" is still one of my least favorite songs. Partly, I just don't like the tune. But on higher reflection, I think I found it hard to internalize the words. Here are the first two verses of the Psalm...

> As a deer longs for flowing streams,
>   so my soul longs for you, O God.
> My soul thirsts for God,
>   for the living God.
> When shall I come and behold
>   the face of God?
>
> — PSALM 42:1-2

While I understood what the Psalm was driving at, and recognized the importance of God in my life, I didn't feel my soul longing for God. I let the language of longing, thirsting, or yearning for God shut down any smaller desire to seek God that may have existed within me. The assumption that everyone who follows Jesus must be longing for a deeper and more intimate relationship with God just didn't ring true to my experience.

Along with the assumption that Christians must want more of God's presence, we have also often assumed that the real problem is somehow related to proper spiritual technique. Books, sermons, blogs, devotionals, and all kinds of other resources have been produced to try to help people connect with God, focusing on the "how-to:" how to pray, how to read the Bible, how to think, how to have more faith. I've preached many such sermons and created my fair share of resources.

This short book of reflections is not a how-to guide. Instead, it is offered as a way of shaking up your thinking about God's presence. I believe it is good and right to want God's presence, but there is something within me that is resistant to that notion. Each part of this book contains reflections on Biblical stories that draw out some of my struggle with the idea of God's presence. I offer this in the hopes that those who struggle with intimacy with God (if you cringed at that phrase, please keep reading—this book is for you!) may have their minds and hearts turned toward a new posture of openness to God's presence.

Of course, there are many people who do have a deep desire within them to enter into God's presence. Perhaps you are one of them. I hope that, as you read these pages, you will find some new ways of thinking about God's presence, and that you will be reminded that there is far more to God's presence than only your personal devotional life.

I want you to know up front that I am not against a "how-to" approach. I think things like resources and devotionals are good and wonderful tools. I do, however, have a problem when I see those resources being used as a way to only approach encounters with God on our own terms, rather than using them to open ourselves up to a divine encounter on God's terms. At the end of this book, I offer a short reflection which is much more how-to focussed, though I don't go very far. Eventually, we must turn to the question of how we can experience God in our lives. My hope is to help you think through the pitfalls we might find ourselves in with "letting God be present."

The first reflection is about God being present with his people in the desert and Moses arguing with God about His continued presence with them on the way to the promised land. In this reflection, we ask whether we are desperate for the presence of God in the same way Moses was. He recognized that their journey would not work without it.

The second part reflects on the story of young Samuel hearing God calling his name in the middle of the night. We sometimes forget that God is present, not recognizing God's voice. There is a greater message in this rich and wonderful story, however. We will explore what happens to us when God chooses to communicate with us and how we learn to listen.

In the third part, we will consider the story of Jesus calming the storm. Here, one of the main features of the story is the fear of the disciples. We will look at how when storms hit, we want God's presence, but in times of calm, we often do not want God. We will look at the story that follows the calm, where Jesus heals a man troubled by an unclean spirit. This man, unlike the disciples, immediately recognizes Jesus for who he really is, and is filled with joy at being changed by Jesus. Do we want God's presence only to have a life that we want, or are we willing to receive a God who moves us into a life of devotion and service?

❧ I ❧
GOD'S PRESENCE EVEN WHEN YOU MIGHT NOT WANT IT

A Reflection on Exodus 31-33

❧ I ❧

GOD'S TANGIBLE PRESENCE

Most of the time, for most of us, God's presence doesn't seem to mean much or matter much. If I'm out playing golf, I'm not thinking about the presence of God. Even in Church meetings, I'm rarely aware of God's presence. When I'm waiting in line at a coffee shop, I'm not really thinking about where God is. God's presence tends to go unnoticed and unacknowledged.

Intellectually, I know God is with me but practically, in the way I live my life, I haven't always acted as though I need God, and I certainly don't feel God's presence at all times. Yet God's presence is immensely important.

In the last few years I have experienced the presence of God more frequently, but I must admit that there have only been three or four times in my life when something quite overwhelming has taken place—where, without any doubt on my part, God was communicating with me in a profound way. Perhaps you have never had such an experience, or perhaps it was so long ago that the memory of it is faded. I've found that the further away in time I get from such experiences, the less impactful they can seem. In the moment they may have been powerful, even life-changing, but in my cynical moments I think, "that was then and this is now." As time passes, and experience makes us jaded, doubt may creep in about whether such experiences were even real.

Many people I know felt closest to God when they were younger, as a teenager or twenty something. They describe times when they experienced God in a tangible way at a camp, or at a conference or rally. These experiences seemed to dry up as other commitments began to encroach: university or college classes, marriage, family, first careers, etc. Even for those who stay committed to Christ, faith often-times can begin to feel lukewarm when it had once been on fire in your youth. What made your faith so alive then, and so hum-drum now?

What's more is that when you haven't had an experience of God in a long time or at all, you may be skeptical of those who claim to hear from God regularly or who get too touchy-feely about the Holy Spirit coming upon them.

Maybe you are someone who would never describe yourself as "spiritual." Maybe you are just an ordinary person who struggles with your faith among the myriad of other life struggles. As life piles up, it can be hard enough to sustain a belief in the existence of God or the plain reality that God is generally present in the world. Actually experiencing God is another matter entirely and feels impossible, perhaps not even desirable anymore.

So, here is the question: do you want God's presence? Not the general, "I know God is always there" presence, but God's presence in a tangible way. Do you want to see evidence of God at work? Do you want to feel or know, deep in your bones, that God is truly with you? I don't know about you, but most days I don't think about it, and on days that I do, I'm lucky if half of the time I would actually answer yes to the above questions.

❦ 2 ❧

COMFORT, CONFRONTATION, AND
AWE-FULL-NESS

Our desire for God's presence can depend on a number of factors, from your mood to the external circumstances of your life.

Sometimes, God's presence means immeasurable comfort. God's presence can mean the difference between life and death, between love and indifference, between the depths of despair and the deepest level of joy. God's presence can mean not being alone when you are at your loneliest. God's presence can mean receiving the strength to continue when life is at its most dire. God's presence, at these times, is something we desperately grasp for, hoping that we can keep hold of it or, better, be held by the One who knows our suffering and struggle.

But sometimes God's presence confronts rather than comforts. Sometimes God's presence makes us keenly aware of being on the wrong track. Sometimes God's presence raises feelings of guilt and shame because we are still holding onto a grudge, or we know we keep hurting people, or we know we've done little caring for others, or we've continued to repeat some other sinful or destructive pattern. God's reminding and confronting presence is usually something we don't want.

God's presence gets described as awesome, but our experience of the presence of God might sometimes be best described as awful. Interestingly, these two words, awesome and awful, both used to mean essentially the same thing. Both originally conveyed a sense of being full of awe or wonder. The word awful (or maybe awe-full) reminds us that our experience of God causes different reactions within us. Sometimes the thought of being with God is too terrible for us—we cannot imagine standing in God's presence. Then, at other times, being with God is the most wonderful, awe-inspiring thing we can know.

✌ 3 ✣

WITH A PARTICULAR PEOPLE

In Scripture, the presence of God is a major theme. God's fundamental promise to His people is that He will be with them as their God. God made this promise initially to Abraham. Along with the promise of His presence, God assured Abraham that he would have many descendants, and one day they would inherit a land to call their own.

That promise seemed lost when the descendants of Abraham found themselves as slaves in Egypt. Under slavery, they worked seven days a week. They suffered, and in their pain, they cried out to God for help.

God raised up Moses, who was commissioned to proclaim the freedom of the chosen people, and lead them out. Moses was reluctant at first but God convinced him, assuring him that signs and wonders would be done and that God would be with him. Moses went to Egypt, and after plagues, signs, and wonders, the King of Egypt allowed the people to be freed.

They went into the desert, ready to journey to the land of promise. They made it to a mountain called Sinai—God's holy mountain. Moses went up and received not just the ten commandments as is often thought, but the entire law and all kinds of other instructions.

These other instructions go into painstaking detail about a few things: the construction of a tabernacle, the clothing of priests, and instructions about how worship ought to take place in the tabernacle.

Moses didn't just receive a moral code on the mountain. He also received a building manual and worship book. This was important, because from this point on, as they travelled, God was going with them, and the tabernacle would be God's home.

The law, all the purity instructions, all the tabernacle descriptions, all the regulations about priests—all of that was designed so that the people would know how to live with God in the midst of their community. Moses received these directives from God so that they would be able to experience and know God's presence daily.

4

IT ALL GOES WRONG

Before Moses went up Mount Sinai, he had been the conduit between God and the people. He spoke for God, sometimes with the assistance of his brother Aaron. When Moses was around, great signs and wonders took place. When Moses was around it was like God was around.

After 40 days and nights on the mountain, God told Moses he had to go back down because the people were sinning. They had forged a golden calf and had decided to worship it instead of God.

Without Moses, it took just forty days to abandon the true God and set up something else to worship. This is first and foremost why an awareness of God's presence is important—because it doesn't take us long to replace God.

God was intensely angry about the people's sin. He told Moses to get off the mountain so He could be left alone in his anger. God also told Moses that he intended to wipe everyone out and start over with just Moses—Moses could be made into a new chosen nation.

This seems out of character for God, but I can kind of understand this reaction. God had had this plan for a really long time.

God had built up the people from Abraham to this point. There had been times of great struggle, but the rescue from Egypt had been the crowning moment where the people would finally understand who God was. God was following through on the promises of old, leading his chosen ones through the desert to establish them in their land flowing with milk and honey.

God had just given Moses all the instructions for how the people would live with God in their midst, and in less than six weeks, the people had pretty much abandoned God. So God was ready to start over.

But something remarkable happened on that mountain. Moses didn't leave God alone to be angry. Instead, Moses talked God down. He interceded. He reminded God of his promise to Abraham and pointed out that the Egyptians would look at things quite differently. The Egyptians, and presumably other nations, would not see a fair God with a righteous anger. They would think that God has evil intentions, leading his people into the desert only for them to die there. God's good name would be hurt in the world at large.

After Moses' intercession, in Exodus 31:14, we read that God changed his mind. God relented and allowed the people to live. He would stay with His people.

With God's assurance to stick with the people, Moses went down the mountain. When he saw what was going on, he was astonished and furious. He smashed the covenant tablets, grabbed the golden calf, melted it down, and once the gold had cooled, he ground it into a powder that he sprinkled into water, which he forced everyone to drink. After that, Moses rallied the Levites to go throughout the camp killing people and three thousand were killed that day.

The story in Exodus 31 hangs there, terrible in our imagination. It is violent and horrific. I don't think this story can be easily explained away and honestly, it is the kind of story that people want to turn away from, or the kind of story that makes people turn away from God, or at least from the Old Testament. So, why mention it here?

I am particularly interested in the conversations between God and Moses. We could just look at those and pretend that the slaughter of the 3,000 never happened but that would be irresponsible. This is part of the Bible and part of the wider story. It was intended to be remembered, to be re-told. The Bible is not condoning what Moses and the Levites did. Exodus does not say that Moses was exacting God's vengeance. Moses acted of his own accord.

Moses went from asking God to be gracious according to His promises, to ordering the slaughter of thousands of his own people in the blink of an eye. Whatever Moses witnessed, in the way people were worshipping the golden calf, must have been a terrible thing to see. My explanation is that Moses lost it. He was exacting and deliberate, but he didn't know what to do with what he witnessed other than mass capital punishment.

Moses' reaction is beyond my imagination, but it does tell me something. It tells me that Moses is fallen just like the people. It tells me that God's chosen people were a mess from day one, and each individual was a mess. We are not talking about each person having a few little problems here. Something far worse and far more depraved is going on.

One of the ways of translating the concept of sin from ancient Hebrew is "missing the mark." I love this understanding because it acknowledges that we try but we don't quite get it. But in this story, right at the high point of Israel's salvation, right as they are receiving the law which becomes the basis for their binding together as a people and to their God, we see something so far past "missing the mark." Sometimes sin is better thought of as atrocity. Human beings don't just "miss the mark." Sometimes we act like monsters.

Whether it is missing the mark or deliberately transgressing, how can we stand in God's presence?

The day after this absolutely horrendous ordeal, God tells

Moses to take the people to the promised land, but tells him: "an angel will go with you, but I won't."

For the rest of their journey there would be no more presence of God. It seems that the people will be literally God-forsaken. And well they should be.

❧ 5 ❧

PRESENCE AS REST

I n Exodus 33:12-13, Moses once again argues it out with God.

While we might think the people, and especially Moses after his genocidal orders, deserve to be forsaken by God, Moses can't imagine going forward through the desert without God's presence on the journey. Moses demands that God reveal the plan to him because he cannot see how anything less than God's presence will work. God told him an angel will guide them, but an angel won't cut it for Moses—it has to be God.

Moses rightly recognizes that the only thing that is sure is God and the promises that God has made. It is precisely at his darkest, most sub-human hour that Moses needs the reassurance that God will not abandon him.

Moses says to God: "You've said you know me by name, and I have found favor in your sight. Now if I have found favor in your sight, show me your ways..." (Exodus 33:12-13). He's basically saying —if we really have a solid relationship, then fill me in on your plan, because I don't see it working!

For good measure, Moses adds, "consider too that this nation is your people." In other words—God, you're responsible for them and I know you care about them!

Like before, God gives in to Moses. In Exodus 33:14, He says, "My presence will go with you, and I will give you rest."

This is such a simple statement for something so significant. Here we get what I believe are the ultimate consequences of God's presence. The Israelites are going to be on a long, wandering journey through the desert. It will be tiring. Every time they camp, they will have to set up this massive tabernacle for God as well as all their own tents. They will do this for forty years. But God says, "I will go with you, and I will give you rest." The primary consequence of God's presence is the people receiving rest.

This is vastly important for the Israelites because of where they have just been. The promise of resting in the presence of God must be understood in the context of the story of their escape from slavery. They had no rest as slaves, that much is obvious, but even the Exodus story to this point has been marked by stressful hurry.

The use of unleavened bread in the Passover celebration illustrates this well. The reason they used unleavened bread was because it was quick to make. The Passover is commemorated with this kind of bread because they left Egypt in big hurry!

After the escape from their oppressors, the Israelites experience hunger and thirst in the desert. We learn that, before the law was given, Moses acted as judge over the people, settling every dispute that arose among the vast numbers of people that were trying to live with one another in makeshift homes. They had no government, no laws, just Moses. His father-in-law advised Moses to appoint others to help him with the easier cases because frankly, Moses was overworked, stressed, and nearing burn-out. It seems there is no rest for the righteous.

The implications of all this haste and hurry play out as the people wait for Moses to come down off the mountain. Haste breeds impatience. The people can't take a break, they can't wait— they forge ahead with their golden calf project.

The people are out of step with the rhythm of creation itself.

The command to rest that Moses will eventually deliver to the people is based on the rest that God took on the seventh day.

All of this context points to the fact that the Sabbath rule is not about regulations, it is really a promise, and here we are reminded that it is intrinsically related to God's presence. It is possible that God gives a command to rest so we can get our own busy-ness, stress, and worry out of the way, in order to experience the presence of the Holy Spirit, and get a glimpse of what the promise of rest is all about.

⚜ 6 ⚜

IT WON'T WORK WITHOUT GOD

A journey like the one before the Israelites was not going to prove particularly restful. Rest, however, is precisely what God promises when He says His presence will go with the people.

Moses continues to argue, however, even though God has already agreed to Moses' request.

> And he said to him, 'If your presence will not go, do not carry us up from here. For how shall it be known that I have found favor in your sight, I and your people, unless you go with us? In this way, we shall be distinct, I and your people, from every people on the face of the earth.'
>
> — EXODUS 33:15-16

This is like Moses saying, "You better mean it, God! Your presence is the only thing that will make this work. I mean, how will we know your favor unless it is really you that is with us? And if you're with us, we will be distinct from everyone else! How awesome is that!"

This last point is important because it is not that they will be distinct in order to be better than, or to beat all the other nations. They will be distinct in order to be a light to the nations. God's presence with them is supposed to make it so that other people see them and understand who the real God is—so that when people see them and the way they live, they will be drawn to the one true God. Moses is saying that without God's presence that just won't happen.

Isn't that the truth?

People are supposed to see us, followers of the living Christ, and be amazed at who the real God is. But if we're not experiencing the presence of God, if we're not thinking about where God is, if we're not aware of God's presence, then others seeing God in us is a pretty unlikely thing.

❧ 7 ❧

WANTING IT

Moses was looking for some assurance from God. He was hoping that God would prove to him that He's serious about going with them. Moses kept arguing because he wanted assurance.

He gets it in Exodus 33:17.

> The Lord said to Moses, 'I will do the very thing that you have asked; for you have found favour in my sight, and I know you by name.'

Moses needed more than the promise of God's presence. He needed to see it, and see it now. He was at the point of really wanting it. He wanted it because he was the one who had to lead the people. He wanted it for his people because he knew they would be the ones who would have to try and live out the holy life of work and rest in God's name, for others to see and be drawn to the most beautiful, wonderful, awe-filled relationship there is. They would need to live this God-filled life. Moses needs more than assurance. He wants the presence of God.

Do we?

YOU CAN'T HAVE AND KNOW
FULLY

 oses wants more and so asks God:

 Show me your glory, I pray.

— EXODUS 33:18

GOD RESPONDS:

 I will make all my goodness pass before you, and will proclaim before you the name, 'The Lord'; and I will be gracious to whom I will be gracious, and will show mercy on whom I will show mercy. But," he said, "you cannot see my face; for no one shall see me and live."

— EXODUS 33:19-20

He tells Moses that His goodness will pass before him and He will proclaim His name to him. He cannot, however, allow Moses to see His face. God can't give Moses everything he wants. Moses can't have full assurance in this life. God establishes Himself as the One who cannot be fully grasped. This is the nature of God, built into the very name of God.

God utters something that we don't know how to say anymore —Yahweh. In most English Bibles, this Hebrew word that was too holy to speak aloud, is replaced by "The LORD." We make that replacement because the Jewish people make the same replacement. Anywhere they see YHWH on the page, they say instead Adonai ("Lord" in Hebrew).

No one quite knows the meaning of God's name, but God gives clues. He says, "I am who I am," which can also mean "I will be who I will be" or even "I exist" or "I am existence."

In this instance, however, when Moses asks to behold God's glory, God plays with His own traditional formula and says: "I will be gracious to whom I will be gracious and will show mercy on whom I will show mercy."

God is in control. God will reveal what God will reveal. God's grace is His to dispense, not ours. God's ways cannot be predicted or controlled by anyone but God. And in the end, God cannot be fully known. Following God, looking for God's presence, seeking God, is never an act of knowing for sure. It is an act of faith.

❧ 9 ❧

DOES IT MATTER TO YOU?

When God threatened to not go with the people, their entire way of life that God had outlined for them would disappear. Moses immediately knew they would be lost without God's presence.

I'm not sure that would happen for most of us. If God wasn't in our lives, would our way of life stop? Would our lifestyle be affected? If the answer is no, and I suspect it is in a lot of ways, we need to think long and hard about that.

If you have made it this far in this chapter, you likely have some sense that God ought to be part of your life. Imagine for a moment if you took God out of the equation of your life completely. What would happen? What would really happen?

For some, this mental exercise makes them give up on faith and the idea of God altogether. Why are we bothering at all, they might say. This exercise convinces them that God isn't really relevant, or that God doesn't make a big difference.

But the problem with giving up on God because He doesn't seem relevant is that we have missed a major warning sign. If God appears irrelevant to your life it may simply mean that your life is more off-track than you want to believe. The thing is, we all, at certain times in our lives, choose to set the true God to one side in favor of much more manageable gods, like our jobs, our families, sports, our own egos.

If you'd ask the Hebrews whether they needed the one true God while Moses was up on the mountain, they would have said "no—we've already made our own god." They were self-sufficient. This should immediately remind us of ourselves.

DETERMINED TO MEET GOD

A beginning place might be to think about the places in your life where the presence of God is more evident. I do not mean for you to think about things like your family or friends, how much they mean to you, and how that must mean that God is present there.

Instead, ask yourself when you really *know* God is present? Where are you when you actually experience God? What kinds of things are you doing? If you can't imagine a time when you do experience God, perhaps there is a time where you feel you are getting close. Maybe there is a time when something is happening, but you aren't quite sure if it is real, or if you believe it, or if you want to let yourself go there.

I want to encourage you to simply start there. Start seeking those times. Perhaps it is during a worship service at church. Perhaps at a Bible study. Maybe when you walk in a park, or when you pray with one or two others, or just when you have a good conversation about spiritual matters. Take a moment and think about it.

From there you can begin to develop more regular practices

that can honestly help you be much more open to the presence of God. You must commit, though, to remembering to want the presence of God.

❦ 11 ❧
GOD'S PRESENCE WITH YOU FOR OTHERS

I f you are like me, wanting the presence of God for yourself may not be much of a motivating factor. My own seeking of God is actually related to the impact that my own God-filled life can have on others.

I hinted at this earlier, but want to make this much more explicit. When God threatened to wipe out his own people, Moses pointed out that this would have a detrimental effect on God's name among other nations. Moses also reminded God about how they needed His presence in order to be a distinct people on the earth.

Part of God's plan for his people has always been for them to be lights to others. Without God's presence in our lives it is near impossible for others to be drawn to God through us, but this is one of God's primary goals for us.

This doesn't mean you need to have it all figured out. As mentioned earlier, seeking and experiencing the presence of God is never an act of knowing for sure. We are called to lives of faith.

What is amazing is that it isn't usually a posture of "knowing everything" about God and God's presence that draws others to God. Rather, it is a posture of trust and faith. People see a deep trust in God and marvel at it, because it is so different from other things we see in our world. The thing is, other people will never accidentally see your trust in God. It must be lived out and put on display.

The ancient Israelites were given all kind of instructions about building a tabernacle, worshiping, and living in a particular way. They were given outward signs in which to participate to remind them of the continual presence of God among them.

We too, must engage in some core practices to help us truly experience the presence of God, the rest that comes with it, and the life-changing nature of it all—not just for us, but for those who see God at work in us.

❧ 12 ❧

TAKE THE EXTRA STEP

I f you are able to think about times when you connect with God, you are already a long way along the path of a growing faith. You are well on your way to God being really present in your life on a regular basis.

You also have something to share with others in your life, because many people know very little about the presence of God.

You are encouraged to take an extra step. Think of someone in your life who you would invite to share in whatever activity you thought of where you come closest to experiencing God's presence. Begin by praying for them. You don't need to tell them you are praying for them. It may be better with some people if you don't tell them. After a bit of praying, invite them along.

This may seem daunting, but think about what you are inviting that person into. You know of a place where you can encounter the Creator of the universe, an activity that helps you experience the presence of One who loves unconditionally. You know how to get in touch with One who befriends sinners and outcasts, addicts and hypocrites. You are a child of an ever-loving Parent and you have a Guide who is also your Brother. You know of One who laid down

His life for you. You have this knowledge and you know people who don't.

As the occasion arises to offer people the opportunity to join you as you seek God, take it. Seize that opportunity to share God's presence with others.

❧ II ❧
TUNING IN AND TRUSTING GOD

A Reflection on 1 Samuel 3

RARELY HEARING FROM GOD

66 ...the word of the Lord was rare in those days.
Visions were not widespread.

— 1 SAMUEL 3:1

I t is interesting that this verse is in the Bible. It is somewhat
unexpected, this admission that we shouldn't expect to
receive visions all the time, and that sometimes the word of
the Lord is rare.

This statement seems counter to much of what is often taught
in church, including what I regularly teach. Preachers tell people
to inquire of the Lord—that God is always speaking and that we
ought to listen. On the flip side, we can be skeptical of those who
claim to hear from the Lord all the time.

From this single statement in First Samuel, we can conclude
two things:

1. Not everyone gets special visions or hears directly from
God. Please note that this does not mean that God
doesn't communicate with us. There are primary ways

God communicates with us that are not particularly "visionary"—through the Bible, in times of prayer, when we take communion, through other people, etc.

2. Some people do get special visions or hear direct words from the Lord. You can't discount that God may be giving you a vision or a direct word.

You might want to ask how you can know if God is trying to tell you something. The answer found in 1 Samuel 3 is this: go and talk to someone about it. In this chapter, Samuel thinks he hears his mentor, Eli, calling him in the middle of the night. Each time Samuel hears his name being called, he runs to Eli and asks what he wants. Eventually, Eli realizes that it is God calling Samuel.

But this passage is deeper than just that simple answer.

❦ 14 ❦

HOPE FOR DWINDLING FAITH

I Samuel 3 is about the dwindling faith of a nation, of a people. This passage speaks to anyone who wishes there were some great vision, or at least a clear word from the Lord, because the time and place they are in is marked by a loss of hope.

Don't listen to the facts of this story. Listen to the mood that's created at the beginning of it.

 Now the boy Samuel was ministering to the Lord under Eli. The word of the Lord was rare in those days; visions were not widespread.

At that time Eli, whose eyesight had begun to grow dim so that he could not see, was lying down in his room; but the lamp of God had not yet gone out, and Samuel was lying down in the temple of the Lord, where the ark of God was.

Then the Lord called, 'Samuel! Samuel!' and he said, 'Here I am!' and ran to Eli, and said, 'Here I am, for you called me.'

— 1 SAMUEL 3:1-6

This passage speaks to those whose faith is like Eli's eyesight: dim and almost gone. But did you hear the hope building in this passage?

Faith has dwindled, but "God's lamp has not yet gone out." God is about to appear again. God is about to do something.

The hope builds, but initially Samuel gets it wrong. He doesn't know it's God calling him. This is where we get hung up, because we want to immediately say—God comes to us as well, and we don't recognize him. That could be true, but it takes all the suspense out of the story. It takes the drama away, it takes the element of hope away. More importantly, it takes God's sovereignty away. We're going to put those elements, drama, hope, and God's sovereignty, back into this story, and hopefully, our lives.

LEARNING TO LISTEN OR LEARNING TO TRUST

This passage is not so much about Samuel getting it initially wrong (and then right) in how to listen to a God who is always speaking. It's about God being in total control even though our human experience often leaves us asking "where is God?"

It's about God knowing exactly what He's doing even when we haven't heard from Him or seen any grandiose visions in a while. This passage isn't about us trying to figure out how to hear God, it's about having faith that God "will do what seems good to Him."

The beginning part of this story builds up hope that God is going to act. He calls Samuel and Samuel thinks it's Eli. Samuel goes to Eli and says, "You called me." Eli says, "No I didn't—go lie down." This happens twice and then we get this:

 Now Samuel did not yet know the Lord, and the word of the Lord had not yet been revealed to him.

— 1 SAMUEL 3:7

Obviously! But look at how the last part is phrased. It doesn't say "he hadn't studied the word of the Lord," or "he wasn't really listening for the Lord," or "he didn't know that God was trying to speak to him." The explanation of why he doesn't recognize God's voice is that a) Samuel didn't yet know God, and b) the word of the Lord had not yet been revealed to Samuel.

This is kind of a weird thing to say. Isn't God trying to reveal his word to Samuel by calling him? Isn't Samuel's basic problem his inability to recognize God?

The phrasing of this verse implies that Samuel's inability to recognize God actually makes sense because *God's word had not yet been revealed.* Even though God had been calling his name, God was not revealing anything to Samuel, at least, not yet. In other words, God calling Samuel by name wasn't really God trying to communicate, at least not in the sense we usually think.

Instead, through his experience that night, Samuel was being educated about who God is. What God was trying to tell him was important, but it was not as important as the experience that God was providing for him.

This might be a bit tricky for us to get our heads around, so let's consider what God didn't do. God could have just woken Samuel up and given him a vision of angels in all glory and power and delivered the message he wanted to give. God could have made it abundantly clear to Samuel who he was, but God didn't do that.

God whispered Samuel's name until Samuel learned that it was God calling him. Why? Because God wasn't just teaching Samuel how to listen. God was teaching him how to trust.

❧ 16 ❧

THE PROCESS IS JUST AS
IMPORTANT AS THE MESSAGE

Sometimes we wish God's will was clear because so often our world makes no sense. Bad things happen to good people, natural disasters happen, we're under stress, we suffer from depression, we struggle in many ways. We wish God would just tell us what to do, or what He is doing.

It's easy to wonder why God doesn't just make life easier, or why God doesn't just explain things to us. But when we jump to that "why God" question, we can miss what God *is* trying to do with us. He may not be giving us visions or speaking audibly His plan for our lives right into our ears, but God is up to something.

Samuel's process of figuring out that God was calling him was just as important as what God was going to tell him. The process built Samuel's faith, allowed him to start to know God, and put him in a position to hear the word that God was going to speak.

Most of us don't like the idea of a process. We'd much rather have an answer. We want to skip ambiguity, avoid difficult questions, do away with life-long learning. We are often unwilling to wait and learn. Most of us are impatient, and we seem particularly impatient with God, who thankfully graces us with His infinite patience.

But we must stick with the path that God puts us on. The process that God works in us is important.

❧ 17 ❧

IT'S UP TO GOD

Eli figures out that it's God who is calling Samuel. Eli's words to Samuel are simple and direct.

> Go lie down and if he calls you, say "Speak, Lord, for your servant is listening."

> — I SAMUEL 3:9

NOTICE THAT ELI SAYS, "IF HE CALLS YOU." ELI DOESN'T presume that God will keep calling Samuel that night. It is entirely God's choice to keep coming back.

Imagine what Samuel was going through when he went back to lie down. He had just been told that the Almighty God had been talking to him and he was to wait for God's voice again. Do you think he fell back asleep? Me neither.

> Now the Lord came and stood there, calling as before.

— 1 SAMUEL 3:10A

This is the first time we read that the Lord came and stood there. Before this verse it was always just God's voice, but now God stands there and calls. Here is the vision. Samuel is now ready for revelation. Samuel finally hears his name and knows who's calling him.

 "Samuel, Samuel."
And Samuel said, "Speak, LORD, for your servant is listening."

— 1 SAMUEL 3:10B

✢ 18 ✢

NOT THE MESSAGE YOU WANTED

We often stop at 1 Samuel 3:10. We like this as an ending. Samuel has learned to listen to God. We learn our simple lesson to always be listening to God's voice, though if this is the only lesson we were intended to learn, we have gained few tools to succeed in it. All we really know is to have a mentor, and check in with him if you hear strange voices in the middle of the night.

We need to move into the next part of 1 Samuel 3 to gain even more from this passage, though this next section is much more difficult.

> Then the Lord said to Samuel, 'See, I am about to do something in Israel that will make both ears of anyone who hears of it tingle. On that day I will fulfil against Eli all that I have spoken concerning his house, from beginning to end. For I have told him that I am about to punish his house for ever, for the iniquity that he knew, because his sons were blaspheming God, and he did not restrain them.

Therefore I swear to the house of Eli that the iniquity of Eli's house shall not be expiated by sacrifice or offering for ever.'

— 1 SAMUEL 3:11-14

Wow! This is bad news. We would expect God to give Samuel a mission, or at least a message of hope to proclaim to God's chosen people. Instead, God tells Samuel about a punishment he is going to dole out on Eli's household.

We are tempted to give up on this story. Surely we can find a less abrasive part of Scripture to learn from: the gospel of John or a Psalm, maybe. Don't give up, though. Stick with it. Remember, it is all part of a process. Don't be tempted by the supposedly easier answers.

> Samuel lay there until morning; then he opened the doors of the house of the Lord. Samuel was afraid to tell the vision to Eli.
>
> — 1 SAMUEL 3:15

No kidding. I'd be terrified to tell Eli what God had just told me. How can Samuel deliver this terrible message to his mentor who had just helped him hear God's voice for the first time?

> But Eli called Samuel and said, 'Samuel, my son.' He said, 'Here I am.' Eli said, 'What was it that he told you? Do not hide it from me. May God do so to you and more also, if you hide anything from me of all that he told you.' So Samuel told him everything and hid nothing from him.
>
> Then he said, 'It is the Lord; let him do what seems good to him.'

And here is the real point of this passage.

Let's think about what we really want in our lives and from God. We may say we want God to give us a vision, to tell us what he wants us to do, or to map out our lives for us. But I think what we'd really like is for God to explain himself to us, or to comfort us, or to fix something for us. We usually want God to work for us. We usually have a very good idea of what we really want to hear from God.

But look what happens when Samuel gets a direct vision from the Lord. When God tells him exactly what He's going to do, it is terrible news. I know my response would be to question God. How can a good God punish Eli for what his kids had done? I'd be angry and disappointed with a message like the one Samuel received.

But Eli tells Samuel, "It is the Lord; let him do what seems good to him." Is Eli's faith misplaced? Has his failing vision finally gone out? Is he resigned to a terrible life? Is he depressed? Does he have no energy to fight anymore? Or does he really believe that it is the Lord and that God is free to do what God feels is best? Is Eli that clear on the fact that only God can be ruler and judge, and that in the end, he and Samuel are but mortals with limited vision? If only we could see as clearly as Eli.

I read this story and I actually stop wanting visions or communication from God, because I don't want bad news. I don't want to be faced with the question of whether I really trust God or not. That's where Samuel was.

God gave him no mission, no task, just a terrible pronouncement about his mentor. And Samuel learned one last lesson from Eli. The lesson of faith even in the face of not understanding what God is doing.

If this story is about anything, it is about how God is going to do what God wants to do. God is going to communicate with you if He chooses. And yes, we can learn things about how to listen for God, but more important and more basic than that, we have to learn to trust God.

In fact, most of God's communication and activity in your life is directed toward building that trust, through challenge and comfort, through joy and struggle.

ꙮ 19 ꙮ

SURPRISE! IT MIGHT NOT BE
ABOUT YOU

The rest of Samuel's growing up story gets summarized at the end of chapter 3.

> As Samuel grew up, the Lord was with him and let none of his words fall to the ground. And all Israel from Dan to Beer-sheba knew that Samuel was a trustworthy prophet of the Lord. The Lord continued to appear at Shiloh, for the Lord revealed himself to Samuel at Shiloh by the word of the Lord. And the word of Samuel came to all Israel.

— 1 SAMUEL 3:19-4:1

SAMUEL BECAME THE MAJOR PROPHET IN ISRAEL. HE WAS THE one who anointed Israel's first kings. It was like he had a direct line to God, forged that night and morning under Eli's supervision. It was built when Samuel decided to truly trust God as his mentor had.

This description at the end of the third chapter points out that it is all about what God is doing, not Samuel. We are told that God "let none of Samuel's words fall to the ground" and that through this, all of Israel recognized Samuel as a trustworthy prophet. We are told further that "the Lord continued to appear, for the Lord revealed himself to Samuel..." It is all God's doing. It is all God's activity.

We are usually very busy worrying about ourselves, and not just in our spiritual lives either. How can I make more money? How can I get a better job? How can I improve my life? How can I have more time for the people and the things I want?

But this passage, which launches one of the most successful prophetic careers in Scripture, is all about what God is doing, and about how God is going to do what seems good to Him.

We are reminded that we were not created for doing our own thing. We were made for glorifying and enjoying God. When we get hung up on ourselves, or even hung up on what action God wants me to take, we start missing what God is doing, and we miss the opportunities to enjoy Him and glorify Him.

You must pay close attention to what God is doing, and allow for the possibility that God's activity is not centred around the life that you are building or have built for yourself. I'm asking you to trust that God will do what He will do and it will include you. God will break into your life. It's not simply a matter of learning good God-listening skills. It's a matter of trusting God with your life.

❧ 20 ❧

MOVING TOWARD GOD WHEN IT IS HARD

As I've reflected on this story about Samuel first hearing God's voice, I've become convinced that a lot of the time we already have an agenda around what we want to hear from God. At the times I want God's presence in my life, it is usually because I want something. It might be comfort or calming in a time of anxiety. It might be healing of some kind. I may hope to gain a sense of direction or I may hope to get an answer to a difficult question.

In essence, I tend to want the presence of God on my own terms. What Samuel discovered is that God will be present on His terms. We tend to try and bend God to our will, when in fact we are supposed to be bending to His.

Samuel's story seems to be about how to be in God's presence and hear His voice. It is about that on one level, but we must be ready to actually allow God to speak. In Samuel's case, God's message was not a welcome one. How will you respond when you hear from God and the message is uncomfortable or disconcerting? Will you trust that God knows what He's doing?

In part one, I tried to help you move from not thinking very much about God's presence to really wanting to be in the presence of God. You may get the impression from this section that I am now moving you further away from God, but that is not my intent. Instead, I am hoping that we can together open our eyes and ears to what God is really saying and doing. My prayer for you is that even when it is hard to hear God, and even more so, when you hear something from God that you don't particularly like, that you will still move toward Him and that you will still trust Him as your God.

In the following section we turn to the story of Jesus calming the storm. There, we will examine more deeply the times when we want God's presence and the times when we don't want it but still need it.

❧ III ❧
AFTER THE STORM
A Reflection On Mark 4:36-41 And What Follows

❦ 21 ❧

MORE THAN THE STORMS OF LIFE

On that day, when evening had come, he said to them, 'Let us go across to the other side.' And leaving the crowd behind, they took him with them in the boat, just as he was. Other boats were with him. A great gale arose, and the waves beat into the boat, so that the boat was already being swamped. But he was in the stern, asleep on the cushion; and they woke him up and said to him, 'Teacher, do you not care that we are perishing?' He woke up and rebuked the wind, and said to the sea, 'Peace! Be still!' Then the wind ceased, and there was a dead calm. He said to them, 'Why are you afraid? Have you still no faith?' And they were filled with great awe and said to one another, 'Who then is this, that even the wind and the sea obey him?'

— MARK 4:36-41

T his is a story about fear and faith. The disciples were on the water in the boat and there was a great storm. It was big enough that they feared for their lives. In a panic, they wake Jesus and accuse him of not caring that they are about to perish on the sea.

Jesus rebukes the wind, rebukes the waves, and rebukes the disciples.

"Why are you afraid?" He asks. "Have you still no faith?"

This story is most often used as a metaphor for life. We have storms in our lives and there is no need to be afraid when you have faith in Jesus.

Just like with Samuel, there is much more to this story, and it has everything to do with the presence of God. In fact, in this story, Jesus is right there with his disciples in the boat. There's just one problem—he's asleep.

❧ 22 ❧

JUST AS HE WAS

We read in verse 36 that the disciples took Jesus with them in the boat "just as he was." What does that mean?

Does it mean Jesus was still wearing the same clothes? Does it mean he didn't wear a life-preserver? Does it mean that they didn't waste any time? Mark is a short gospel—why include this phrase at all?

I think it is included to emphasize that they didn't take a different Jesus. He was about to do something remarkable, but he is still Jesus, the man. He's the teacher and the healer you've been hearing about. There is nothing up his sleeve. There is no trick to the story about to follow.

❧ 23 ❧

OTHER BOATS WERE WITH HIM

Another strange phrase to note in this story is the mention that "other boats were with him."

This story is not just about the disciples.

Here is perhaps a lesson just as important as the idea that Jesus can calm the storms of "my life" – there are others out in the storm.

When the disciples raise their complaint to Jesus about him not caring, it's not just about them. It is also about whether Jesus cares about all the other boats out on the water.

We ought to relate to this. Even though a lot of our daily concerns center around ourselves, we don't only ask about where God is in the storms of our own personal lives. We also ask whether God cares about the millions dying of cancer. We wonder about God's presence when a natural disaster kills innocent people. We ask why God doesn't do something about terrorism, domestic violence, or the slave trade. Our storms as a human race are pretty big, and we naturally ask, does God care? Those are bigger questions than our own personal storms. There were other boats on the water.

❧ 24 ❧

IF YOU HAD REAL FAITH

The storm itself is the easy part to fit into our usual metaphor of "the storms of life." We can picture what those storms might be and we've already named some in the section above. We could make all kinds of lists of potential storms, including: relationship troubles, stress at work or in school, bullying, substance abuse or other addictions, etc.

We immediately get the metaphor of the storm and we understand the fear of the disciples. We can feel equally overwhelmed.

I supposed Jesus being asleep portrays the way we sometimes feel. Jesus is supposed to be at the wheel, steering us through the storms, but so often it feels as though we have lost our rudder or that no one is in control. The complaint of the disciples fits perfectly. They give voice to exactly how we feel when we are being crushed in the storms of life. God, don't you care?

What is fascinating to me in the way Mark tells this story, is that the words "afraid" and "faith" only get used after the disciples wake Jesus up. I have continued to point to the fact that the disciples are fearful, but we do not get confirmation of this until Jesus finally gets up and speaks. It is, in fact, Jesus, not the narrator or the disciples, that first uses the words "afraid" and "faith."

There are several ways we can understand Jesus' words: "Why are you afraid? Have you still no faith?" (Mark 4:40)

One possibility is that Jesus is telling them that if they had real faith they would have just ridden out the storm, trusting that God would see them through. Jesus calming the storm is a sign of what God is capable of. They should have trusted in God's protection because God has complete control.

A second possibility is that Jesus is telling them that if they had real faith, they would have prayed for God to calm the storm and God would have done it. Jesus calming the storm is a sign of what any of the disciples, if they had faith, could have done. The prayer offered in faith can move God to miraculous action.

We're going to explore a third possibility...

❧ 25 ❧

MUZZLE IT

When Jesus refers to the fear of the disciples and their lack of faith, he might not be referencing the storm at all. Rather, he might be talking about the calm that follows the storm.

Imagine being in the middle of the storm and you are an accomplished fisherman. You've seen your fair share of storms. You start out doing all the things you know how to do. You struggle against the storm, you bail out water, you act quickly, but, ultimately, you realize you are stuck out there. You look over and see Jesus, who is by no means a boatman, asleep. How can someone sleep through this?

It becomes clear that there is no hope. Certainly, you are afraid of death at sea, but you're more angry that your teacher, the one you gave up fishing for, is sleeping. You're now at the moment where he is needed—the moment before it's all over. You're not really expecting him to do anything to keep the boat afloat, but if anyone could prepare you to meet your Maker it would be him. You wake him up with an accusation: "don't you care that we're perishing?"

He woke up and rebuked the wind, and said to the sea, 'Peace! Be still!' Then the wind ceased, and there was a dead calm.

— MARK 4:39

A better translation of what Jesus said might be "Silence! Muzzle it!" The text tells us that Jesus spoke to the sea, but imagine you're the disciple who woke him up with "don't you care?" and that's when Jesus gets up and shouts out to everyone and everything "Silence! Muzzle it!" And everyone and everything obeys, everything stops, and there's nothing but calm.

I think the calm that followed Jesus' command is far more likely to be the moment of the greatest fear for the disciples. It is a moment that takes your breath away.

✥ 26 ✥

WHAT MANNER OF MAN IS THIS?

> He said to them, 'Why are you afraid? Have you still
> no faith?'
>
> — MARK 4:40

Jesus knows they're afraid, but *why* are they afraid? And why does Jesus accuse them of having a lack of faith? Verse 41 fills us in.

> And they were filled with great awe and said to one
> another, 'Who then is this, that even the wind and
> the sea obey him?'
>
> — MARK 4:41

"GREAT AWE" IS FROM THE GREEK WORD *PHOBON* AND IT USUALLY
means the outward expression of fear, panic, or flight. In other

words, Jesus can see that what they really want to do is run away in panic after what they just witnessed.

It is then that the disciples say to each other, "Who then is this?" or, as the King James version put it, "What manner of man is this?"

Remember the detail from the beginning? They took him on the boat "just as he was." Now they ask, "What manner of man is this?"

In our English Bibles this sentence gets rendered in such a way that it sounds like Jesus has got them in awe, wondering who he could be. But the Greek can easily be read as them trembling in fear of a man who can wield supernatural powers. What kind of human being can do things like this? The obvious answer is—a human being can't.

Perhaps the disciples are much more afraid of Jesus himself and the calm that He produced. "What manner of man is this?" is a question that is slightly off kilter, because Jesus is not simply a human being, he is not just a man. He is God with them. This story is all about the presence of God. The disciples brought him along "just as he was," they just didn't know who he really was.

And so, the third possibility for understanding Jesus' words about fear and faith is this: "If you had real faith you would recognize that the incredible miracle that just took place was from God and God is right there with you." Jesus calming the storm is a sign of what God does all the time at will. It is not a sign of what God will do *only if* we have enough faith, or what God is *capable* of doing to protect us every time we're in trouble. The calming of the storm is a miracle of power that points to the power of Jesus who is God. We either fear Him as a human being, or trust Him as God.

✶ 27 ✶

CHANGED BY THE CALM

W e tend to universalize this story. The storm represents our struggles and our trials, and we just have to have faith, as though this was a simple answer to all the world's problems. What if instead we only universalized the calm after the storm, and did so to remind ourselves of the source of the miraculous, the source of healing, reconciliation, comfort, peace, of every good and transforming gift?

There *are* remarkably good things that happen in our lives. Sometimes they are striking, like a friend going into remission and it baffles the doctors. Sometimes we call these things miracles. But less and less do we see them connected to God. And even less than that, will we tell people that it is God who worked the miracle? Only in the rarest of cases will we let the miracle have a lasting positive effect on our faith in God. That is because, as we will see, in the calm that follows a storm, there is still an undercurrent of fear.

It's not just a fear of Jesus that the disciples had, but a fear of what would be next with this Jesus. In the middle of the storm, they had jobs to do, they had to work hard. When there was no hope of survival, they could at least cry out "Don't you care, Jesus?"

But when Jesus turned things around, there is only the unknown after that.

We might think we fear the storm, but life is full of lots of storms. Some are overwhelming, but lots of them are just draining. It's the calm that God provides afterwards that can really transform us. And for lots of us that is the real fear: that God who is in the midst of the storm and who brings the ensuing calm will change us. We're afraid of that because quite often, we don't really want to be changed.

28

NOT WANTING CHANGE

We've all known people, or have at least heard stories about people, who have had a brush with death and then had their life transformed. You know the one about the guy who has a heart attack, survives, and then vows to live differently afterward.

I don't know if these kinds of stories are inspirational. Maybe they are, maybe they aren't. I don't know if this scenario is instructive either. It could be, I suppose. What I do know is that most of us don't actually want to go through this kind of journey. We don't want to live through a storm even if we know we will be changed for the better on the other side.

Maybe I'm off base here, but most of the time, I don't really want to be different than I am. I don't want God to go to work on me, using circumstance or miracles to push me to live differently.

I'm somewhat content. Not everything is perfect. Life could be better, yes, but it's pretty good. And the things I want to be different in life are not really about me. I'd like a little more money, less car repairs to do, more vacations, and more time with my family. A whole new life transformed by God through a storm and an ensuing calm? I'm not so sure about that.

I suppose what I am spiralling around here is this: I want God to show up when I need Him. I'm just like the disciples in the boat. When the storm is strongest, I want God's presence. It doesn't take too long after the storm calms down for me to not really want God around anymore. I suppose if I'm honest, I have a healthy fear of the storm, but an unhealthy fear of God.

I'm fine when God calms the storms around me. I'm thankful for it. It is God's presence in the following stillness that scares me. What will God do now? And what will God ask me to do? When we've been moved beyond survival, suddenly we may be confronted with God's call to service, and God's penchant for personal transformation. I'd rather just go back to fishing on the lake.

But Jesus saves us *for* something. He doesn't leave us as merely saved from our storms or sins to live as we did before. He plants purpose in us and changes us more into his likeness. This is scary because if we are being changed into his likeness, then we are walking a path of service and suffering as he did.

I may be over thinking this here, but I believe all of these thoughts are in play. If I'm honest, quite often I don't want a wholly other life defined by the one who is wholly Other. Left to my own devices, I would much rather have a life defined by the successes and trappings of our world. Yes, save me from the storm, Jesus. But only so that I can go to Starbucks and have my seven dollar coffee, and at the end of a long day settle in for some Netflix binge-watching.

Our usual response to the calm after the storm is not a particularly faithful response. It is to "get my life back" rather than "give my life to." So how does the person of faith respond to the calm after the storm?

29

ALLOW YOURSELF TO BE WITH JESUS

The person who has no faith will panic and worry about the miraculous calm and what may happen next. The person of faith will trust that God has provided the calm and God will do the changing, so they will do their best to cooperate with what God has done and what God is going to do.

The story that follows this one in Mark illustrates this very point.

Jesus goes into a Gentile region. There is a man there that is kept chained up in a graveyard and he has an unclean spirit. His chains can't hold him, he continually breaks them. It's a pretty creepy scene. When he sees Jesus, he runs to him and shouts, "What have you to do with me, Jesus, Son of the Most High God? I adjure you by God, do not torment me." (Mark 5:7)

Notice that the unclean spirit in the man, or perhaps even the man himself, recognizes Jesus as the Son of God. The disciples just asked "What manner of man is this?" after an incredible miracle. This demon-possessed mad-man has no problem pinpointing Jesus' true identity.

I find it interesting that the hand-picked disciples, the good upstanding fishermen, the faithful religious ones who have experienced the miraculous, have trouble working out who Jesus is, but not the irreligious demon-possessed man, chained up in a graveyard. Jesus goes right to the one everyone would avoid, and somehow that one knows him.

Jesus ends up healing the man. After being healed, he starts following Jesus and asks Jesus if he can come with him on the boat, just to be with him.

Notice what happens to the man. He isn't afraid like the disciples. He is bold enough to follow Jesus. He immediately knows where he wants to be—with the one who healed him. He correctly associates his new life with the one who has given it. He is changed and he embraces it.

Jesus says no to the man's request, but tells him instead to go home and tell his friends how much God has done for him. We find out that he did just that, giving all of the credit to Jesus. The text tells us that everyone was amazed.

Our experience of Jesus, our encounter with the calm after the storm, God bringing some order into our chaotic lives, is supposed to be met with the faith that this man displayed, not with the paralyzed fear of the disciples on the boat. A lot of the time, we get scared about the calm, about suddenly not having a job to do, about Jesus having given us a beautiful gift, about him changing the circumstances. We get scared because Jesus may be changing us in the process. We get scared because in the end we don't really want to be changed.

Instead, can we be faithful? Can our first response be to desire His presence? Can we follow Him, and want to be around Him?

Let's not let the miraculous, when we encounter it, perplex and paralyze us. Instead, let's instantly credit Jesus, and connect whatever goodness and transformation we experience with its source— our Lord God: Father, Son and Spirit. Perhaps then we will be moved to go and tell about Jesus and what He has done for us, so that all will be amazed.

❧ IV ❧
SO, WHAT NOW?

❦ 30 ❧
EXPERIENCING GOD MORE CONSISTENTLY

I began by assuring you that this book was not a how-to guide. Perhaps, though, you have become a little more aware of some of the times when you close yourself off to the presence of God. You likely have times when you don't think about God's presence, or when you don't want it because God confronts you, challenges you, changes you, or simply doesn't do what you want Him to do.

But what if you have decided that you do want to experience God more? What if you are ready to accept God on His terms? Maybe you want to trust God to be the one in charge of your encounter with Him regardless of how that encounter turns out.

If you are in this place, I'm thrilled. It took me a long time to get to a place of wanting more encounters with God. I still have moments when I ignore God, but they are less frequent now. Mostly, this is because when I have sought experiences of God, the times of comfort and joy have far outweighed the times of challenge.

Even as I write this, I know I am not being entirely accurate. I think it is more that my experience of God tends to have an under-current of joy and a sense of being loved. Even in times of challenge or change that I don't feel like I want, there is this joy, or what the Apostle Paul calls, "the peace that passes understanding." (Philippians 4:7)

A big part of this undercurrent of joy has been sustained through the daily reading of Scripture and daily prayer. I think as well, the kind of prayer and the method of reading the Bible matters. Each morning I pray, "Holy Spirit, come, and fill me with your joy" or some other similar, simple prayer. I attempt to read the Bible slowly for understanding and encounter, and not to meet a goal. I struggle with the last one because I am a goal oriented person. I like to check off that I've read five chapters a day. But when I go for some time reading Scripture without a goal of completion in mind, I find that in the reading I am simply more open to God and the peace that comes from experiencing His presence.

In recent years I have taken to prayer walking. During these times I almost always pray questions and listen for God's answers. Usually, the questions are something like, "God what do you want me to do?" or "what do you have in store for me?" I try to keep these prayer times as relatively agenda-less. I resist asking about specific problems. I don't ask, "God what do you want me to do about ____?" I try to allow God to direct me. The metaphor of walking is helpful here. Often I don't know the exact path I will go, but I trust. In the same way, I trust that God will show up and lead me in times of prayer.

I don't always "feel" the presence of God in my prayer times, but since I became more consistent, I have encountered God's presence far more. Since I started paying attention to letting go of my own agenda in Scripture reading and prayer, I've felt much more as though God is with me.

Not all of these practices will work for you, and you may find some of your own, but in the end we are talking about a relationship, and that is the way relationships are. Unique in every case. I say all this in the hope that you will know that God's presence in your life is possible and even desirable. Much of this book can be summed up by saying the way to let God be present is to try and get yourself out of the way. That isn't particularly practical however.

There are practical helps to experiencing God's presence, but I've found that most of them come down to establishing consistent daily and weekly patterns in which you regularly seek to connect with God. What is the place of daily prayer and Scripture reading for you? What is the nature of your prayer? Do you spend time listening to God?

I don't ask these questions to cause guilt for those times when you are not praying or reading the Bible consistently. Rather, I pray that you will be encouraged to seek God out.

You may, like me, be someone who never really wanted an "intimate relationship with God," but the reality is that there is a relationship and it will look different for you than it does for others. You may not ever use words like "longing for God's presence," but God is still showing up in your life. Will you lean in and listen? Will you leave fear behind and trust instead?

Will you let God be present?

THANKS FOR READING

It means so much to me that you have taken the time to read *Let God Be Present*. If you found it helpful, please consider helping to spread the word about this book by doing one the following:

- Leave a rating and review on Amazon - This really helps books get seen by other readers, and means a ton to me as an author - I really do notice it and appreciate the support!
- Tell someone about it, or buy it for someone. You can tell someone on social media, by email, or just in person.
- Email me at matt@mattbrough.com and let me know what you think. I really love hearing from readers, and it also helps me know what kinds of things to include in future books!

OTHER LET GOD BOOKS

Let God Be God

When our desires and God's will don't match up, we often choose to move God from the center of our life to just being an "important part" of it. This book will challenge you to think differently about what it means to have faith. It asks you to set yourself aside, make God your true focus, and trust God to truly be God in your life.

❧

Let God Send

Crossing Boundaries and Serving in Christ's Name

God sends each follower of Jesus to serve others. The way we serve might be in small and simple ways, but God also tends to stretch us, moving us beyond the easy and across boundaries that we wouldn't always wish to cross. Not a how-to guide, this book is a thought provoker for anyone serious about following Christ, who wonders how to keep serving over a lifetime of faith.

74671806R00048

Made in the USA
Columbia, SC
07 August 2017